W9-CLU-402

Nature Basics

Living and Nonliving

by Carol K. Lindeen

Consulting Editor: Gail Saunders-Smith, PhD

Consultant: Sandra Mather, PhD
Professor Emerita of Geology and Astronomy
West Chester University, Pennsylvania

Capstone press
Mankato, Minnesota

Pebble Books are published by Capstone Press,
151 Good Counsel Drive, P.O. Box 669, Mankato, Minnesota 56002.
www.capstonepress.com

Printed in the United States of America

1 2 3 4 5 6 12 11 10 09 08 07

Library of Congress Cataloging-in-Publication Data

Lindeen, Carol, 1976–

Living and nonliving / by Carol K. Lindeen.

p. cm.—(Pebble Books. Nature basics)

Includes bibliographical references and index.

ISBN-13: 978-1-4296-0000-2 (hardcover)

ISBN-10: 1-4296-0000-4 (hardcover)

1. Life (Biology)—Juvenile literature. I. Title. II. Series.

QH501.L56 2008

570—dc22 2006101948

Summary: Simple text and photographs present living and nonliving things.

Note to Parents and Teachers

The Nature Basics set supports national science standards related to earth and life science. This book describes and illustrates living and nonliving things. The images support early readers in understanding the text. The repetition of words and phrases helps early readers learn new words. This book also introduces early readers to subject-specific vocabulary words, which are defined in the Glossary section. Early readers may need assistance to read some words and to use the Table of Contents, Glossary, Read More, Internet Sites, and Index sections of the book.

Table of Contents

Living and Nonliving

The world is full of living and nonliving things. Frogs are living things. They breathe, eat, grow, and move.

Rocks are
nonliving things.
Rocks are
made of minerals.

What Living Things Do

Living things act in different ways than nonliving things. Living things grow and change.

gills

Living things breathe.
Fish breathe
through gills.

4961

Living things need food.
Cows eat plants.
Plants make their
own food from sunlight,
water, and soil.

Living things move
on their own.
Flowers turn toward sunlight.
Watering cans can't
move on their own.

Living things react
to changes around them.
Dogs chase balls.
Balls can't see
or hear dogs.

Living things grow older and die. Leaves grow and change color. Then they fall to the ground.

Alive or Not Alive?

Farms are full of living and nonliving things. Which things are living? Which things are nonliving?

Glossary

breathe—to take in air

gills—the organs on a fish's side that it uses to breathe; sharks breathe through gills.

mineral—a solid in the ground made by nature that is not a plant or animal; minerals are found in rocks and soil.

react—to do something in response to another action

Read More

Hewitt, Sally. *Living Things: Is It Alive?* Science Starters. North Mankato, Minn.: Stargazer Books, 2007.

Royston, Angela. *Living and Nonliving.* My World of Science. Chicago: Heinemann Library, 2003.

Internet Sites

FactHound offers a safe, fun way to find Internet sites related to this book. All of the sites on FactHound have been researched by our staff.

Here's how:

1. Visit *www.facthound.com*
2. Choose your grade level.
3. Type in this book ID **1429600004** for age-appropriate sites. You may also browse subjects by clicking on letters, or by clicking on pictures and words.
4. Click on the **Fetch It** button.

FactHound will fetch the best sites for you!

Index

Word Count: 132
Grade: 1
Early-Intervention Level: 14

Editorial Credits
Erika L. Shores, editor; Ted Williams, designer; Jo Miller, photo researcher

Photo Credits
Bruce Coleman Inc./Gail M. Shumway, cover (frog); Masa Ushioda/V&W, 10
Corbis/zefa/Anna Peisl, 14
Dreamstime.com/Joeshmo, 18
fotolia/Kerioak, 16
Getty Images Inc./The Image Bank/Bob Elsdale, 4
iStockphoto/Amy Burgess, 8; Dan Bailey, 20
Shutterstock/Johan Swanepoel, 1; Kurt De Bruyn, 12; Martin Bowker, 6; Nicola Gavin, cover (rock)